Magic Tricks with Cards

Elsie Olson

Lerner Publications ◆ Minneapolis

Lerner Publications Company
A division of Lerner Publishing Group, Inc.
241 First Avenue North
Minneapolis, MN 55401 USA

For reading levels and more information, look up this title at www.lernerbooks.com.

Library of Congress Cataloging-in-Publication Data

Names: Olson, Elsie, 1986- author.
Title: Magic tricks with cards / Elsie Olson.
Other titles: Tricks with cards
Description: Minneapolis, Minnesota : Lerner Publications Company, [2019] | Series: Lightning Bolt Books — Magic tricks | Includes bibliographical references and index. | Audience: Ages: 6-9. | Audience: Grades: K to Grade 3.
Identifiers: LCCN 2018011215 (print) | LCCN 2018018831 (ebook) | ISBN 9781541543386 (eb pdf) | ISBN 9781541538948 (library binding : alk. paper)
Subjects: LCSH: Card tricks—Juvenile literature. | Magic tricks—Juvenile literature.
Classification: LCC GV1549 (ebook) | LCC GV1549 .O57 2019 (print) | DDC 793.8/5—dc23

LC record available at https://lccn.loc.gov/2018011215

Manufactured in the United States of America
1-45077-35904-6/15/2018

Table of Contents

Getting Started

Have you ever watched a magician perform? There is a secret behind every trick. Magicians perform tricks using playing cards. With practice, you can do card tricks too!

Card Trick Tips

- **Practice!** It can take a long time to perfect a trick. Practice in front of a mirror until you are ready.

- **Make the cut.** Card tricks often call for cutting the deck. To do this, remove a portion of the cards off the top of the deck. Restack the deck with the cut portion on the bottom or as instructed.

- **Fan out right.**

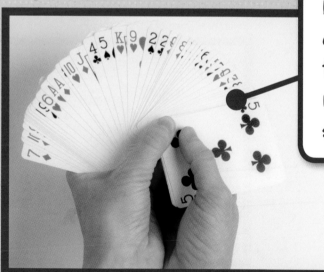

During tricks, always fan out the cards to the right so you can see the numbers.

- **Make the trick your own!** Add a magic word, tell a story, or find another way to make the trick unique.

Not So Tricky

Magic Card Finder

Use a tricky flip to magically pick a secret card!

What you need:

- Deck of playing cards
- Audience helper

Getting ready:

Stack the cards. Make sure they are all facedown. Flip the bottom card over.

The trick:

1. Fan out the cards facedown. Keep the bottom card hidden.

2. Ask your helper to choose a card. Tell her to remember it but not to show you.

3. Restack the deck. Secretly flip the deck over while your helper memorizes the card. *Now the bottom card is on top!*

4. Have your helper slide her card back into the deck.

5. Pass the deck from one hand to the other behind your back. As you do so, flip the deck back over.

6. Tell your helper that her card will reveal itself in the deck. Then fan out the cards for the audience.

Your helper's card will be the only one facing the wrong way!

Odd Card Out

Mystify your friends by picking the odd card out!

What you need:

- Deck of playing cards
- Audience helper

Getting ready:

Sort the deck into two piles. One will have cards with odd numbers and the other will have cards with even numbers. Put one pile on top of the other, so it looks like a regular deck.

Queens and aces go into the even cards pile. Put the jacks and kings into the odd cards pile.

The trick:

1. Divide the deck into two even stacks.

The stacks will be sorted by odd and even cards. It's OK if a few cards get into the wrong stack.

2. Ask your helper to draw a card from the middle of one stack and memorize it. But don't let him show it to you!

3. While your eyes are closed, have your helper place the card into the middle of the other stack.

4. Flip through the second stack until you find the card that doesn't belong. Show your helper his card!

A Little Tricky

Mind Reader

Make your friends believe you can read their minds!

What you need:

- Deck of playing cards

The trick:

1. Fan out the cards face-up for your audience. Memorize the card farthest to the left.

2. Restack the deck facedown. Cut the deck and place the cut cards face-up on top of the deck.

3. Cut the deck again. Make sure your second cut is deeper than the first cut. Flip the cut cards to place them face-up on top of the deck.

4. Remove the face-up cards from the top of the deck. Take the first facedown card and show it to the audience without looking at it. This will be your memorized card from step 1!

5. Tell everyone you are reading their minds. Then say the card you memorized in step 1!

Card Whisperer

Thrill your audience when a playing card tells you its secrets.

What you need:

- Deck of playing cards
- Audience helper

The trick:

1. Let your helper mix up the cards. Fan out the deck face-up to show your audience the cards are in a random order. As you do this, memorize the third card from the left.

Third card from the left

2. Restack the deck, and shuffle or mix the cards one more time. But be sure to keep the top three cards together at the top of the deck. *Your memorized card will be in the same position.*

3. Let your helper cut the deck, but do not restack.

4. Take a jack, queen, or king card from the bottom half of the deck. Explain that this card is going to tell you the third card in the other stack.

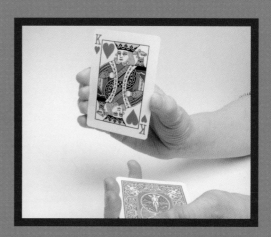

5. Say your memorized card. Then flip over the first three cards in the top half of the deck.

The third card will be the one you memorized!

Magic Card Order

Stun your audience when you correctly guess how many cards they secretly moved.

What you need:

- Ace, joker, and one each of cards two through ten of any suit
- Audience helper

Getting ready:

Stack the cards in this order, from top to bottom: 6, 5, 4, 3, 2, ace, joker, 10, 9, 8, 7.

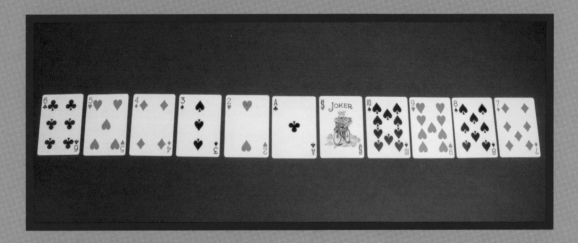

The trick:

1. Lay out the cards face-down in a row from left to right. Have your helper stand next to you.

2. Ask your helper to move one or more cards from the right side of the row to the left side. Turn your back so you can't see her move them. Tell her to remember how many cards she moved.

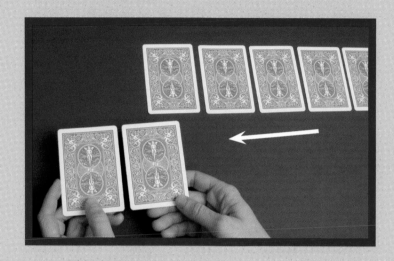

3. When your helper is finished, turn back around. Tell her you can guess how many cards she moved.

4. Count in from the left side of the row and flip over the seventh card. The card will show the number of cards your helper moved. If she didn't move any cards, you will flip over the joker. If she moved one card, you will turn over the ace.

Terrifically Tricky

Magic Speller

Surprise your audience by spelling out a secret card!

What you need:

- Deck of playing cards
- Audience helper

The trick:

1. Ask your helper to choose a card but not let you see it. Meanwhile, secretly peek at the card on the bottom of the deck and memorize it.

This will be your marker card.

2. Have your helper place his card on top of the deck. Then have him cut the deck in half.

3. Fan out the deck. Say you need a moment to read the cards. *Your marker card is now to the left of your helper's secret card.*

4. Starting with your marker card as number one, count out five cards from right to left, one for each letter of the word *magic*.

5. Take the remaining cards to the left of the fifth card and turn them facedown. Restack the rest of the deck facedown on top of them.

6. Flip over the cards one at a time as you spell out *m-a-g-i-c*. Say one letter with each card. When you have finished spelling, the next card you flip over will be your helper's secret card!

The Mysterious Jumping Card

Delight your fans with a magical jumping card!

What you need:

- Deck of playing cards
- Audience helper

Getting ready:

Practice steps 2 and 3 over and over again before doing this trick for an audience.

The trick:

1. Ask your helper to draw any card from the deck. Look at the card and show it to the audience. Then bring the card and the deck behind your back.

2. Behind your back, slip the card just beneath the top card in the deck.

3. Show the audience the deck. Draw the top two cards. Hold them with your fingers placed on the top and bottom edges of the cards. This will make it look as if you are just drawing one card.

4. Show that you are holding your helper's card. Then place the two cards back on top of the deck.

5. Ask your helper to move the top card to anywhere in the deck.

6. Knock on the deck and say, "Jump!" Then flip over the top card. It will look as if your helper's card magically moved back to the top!

Card Trick Tidbits

- A standard deck of playing cards has fifty-two cards plus two jokers. The fifty-two cards are divided into hearts, diamonds, spades, and clubs.

- Playing cards have been around since at least the tenth century CE. The first cards were invented in China.

- In the late nineteenth century, magician Harry Houdini called himself the King of Cards. He could make cards seem to appear out of thin air!

Meet a Magician!

Ricky Jay

Ricky Jay is considered by many to be the best card trick magician in the world. Jay was born in Brooklyn, New York, in 1948. He performed his first magic trick in public at the age of four. As an adult, he earned a world record for throwing a playing card 190 feet (58 m). The card traveled at 90 miles (145 km) per hour!

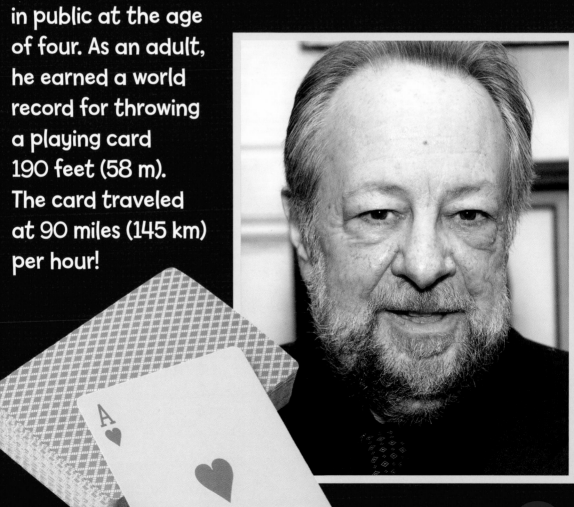

Glossary

magician: a person who performs magic tricks

memorize: to learn something with the goal to remember it

mystify: to confuse or puzzle

shuffle: to mix up the order of the cards in a deck

unique: unlike anything else that has been done

Further Reading

Funology — Four Robbers Card Trick
http://www.funology.com/four-robbers/

Higginson, Sheila Sweeny. *Pulling Back the Curtain on Magic.* New York: Simon Spotlight, 2015.

Jay, Joshua. *Big Magic for Little Hands.* New York: Workman Pub., 2014.

Kelly, Kristen. *Abracadabra! Fun Magic Tricks for Kids.* New York: Sky Pony Press, 2016.

Kidspot — Four Aces Magic Trick
http://www.kidspot.com.au/things-to-do/activity-articles/four-aces-magic-trick/news-story/98767368922152b9e0ae1255c3290f0f?ref=collection_view,magic-tricks

Magic Tricks for Kids — Color Changing Card Magic Trick
http://magictricksforkids.org/color-changing-card-magic-trick/

Index

Photo Acknowledgments

The images in this book are used with the permission of: © Shutterstock, pp. 2, 20, 21 (left);
© iStockphoto, p. 4; © Mighty Media, Inc., pp. 5, 6, 7, 8, 9 (top), 9 (bottom), 10, 11 (top),
11 (bottom), 12, 13 (top), 13 (bottom), 14, 15 (top), 15 (bottom), 16, 17 (top), 17 (bottom), 18,
19; © Getty Images, p. 21 (right).

Front cover: © Shutterstock.

Main body text set in Billy Infant.